The Art of the
Cocktail

100 Classic Cocktail Recipes

Philip Collins

Photography by Sam Sargent

CHRONICLE BOOKS ~ SAN FRANCISCO

A Fillip Book
Copyright © 1992 by Fillip Films, Inc. Photography © 1992 by
Sam Sargent. All rights reserved. No part of this book may be
reproduced in any form without written permission from the
publisher.

Printed in Hong Kong.

Library of Congress Cataloging-in-Publication Data
Collins, Philip, 1944
      The Art of the cocktail : 100 classic cocktail recipes /
Philip Collins ; photography by Sam Sargent.
          p.   cm.
     Includes index
     ISBN 0-8118-0154-3 (pbk.)
     1. Cocktails.   I. Title.
     TX 951.C725   1992   92-1264
     641.8'74—dc20   CIP

Drink Styling by Steve Shern and Alison Sklute

Editing: Chuck Robbins
Book and Cover Design: Blue Design
Cover Photograph: Sam Sargent

Distributed in Canada by
Raincoast Books
8680 Cambie Street
Vancouver, B.C. V6P 6M9

10 9 8 7 6

Chronicle Books
85 Second Street
San Francisco, California 94105

The recipes contained in this book call for brand names which
are registered trademarks. The proprietors of these brand names
have not endorsed the recipes.

Other Fillip Books by Philip Collins from Chronicle Books:
Radios: The Golden Age
Radios Redux
Smokerama: Classic Tobacco Accoutrements

Table of Contents Illustration:
A selection of miniatures containing popular brands used in
mixing these classic cocktails.

The Art of the

Cocktail

For my Kay.

Contents:

Introduction

Cocktail — The word itself reverberates, echoing an earlier era and evoking an idyllic setting complete with sophisticated men in dinner jackets and glamorous women in little black dresses. It is a word suffused with images of mystery, wit, repartée, even love.

To order a cocktail is to enter another world, a time before the advent of pallid white wines and designer mineral waters, before drunk-driving tests and rigid concerns about the effect of alcohol upon the citizenry's health. A cocktail is a statement and a sign of awareness and knowledge, of adult sensibilities and concerns and pleasures. To drink a cocktail is to partake of nuance and memory. Evocative and subtle, the cocktail becomes the centerpiece in a ritual of release, a beverage to be consumed at virtually any hour and at every level of society. But above all, the cocktail is a social device. The fundamental requirement of the cocktail is that it enhance pleasant surroundings, good company, and sparkling conversation.

Although there is no denying the cocktail's allure and satisfaction, it is, in a sense, merely an excuse. The formalities of alcohol mix and glassware are simply the bedrock upon which to build the larger experience: the cocktail hour, a time as important as the beverage itself, when people gather with friends, to savor the small victories of the day, to laugh, to reaffirm themselves. Obviously, the cocktail hour may be enjoyed virtually anywhere. A cocktail lounge is appropriately ideal, but the local saloon, a beach-front deck, or an airliner seat will suffice. For many people, the cocktail is taken at home. Here, after returning from the daily work routine and before embarking upon the evening's duties, a brief hiatus is carved from the busy day.

The Art of Mixing — Because the cocktail and its attendant rituals are so important in maintaining a balance in busy lives, a little attention paid to a few details concerning the making of cocktails will increase your enjoyment.

Supplies
- A few basic bottles of liquor should suffice: scotch, vodka, bourbon, brandy, gin, sweet and dry vermouth.
- Include ice, half-and-half, bitters, tomato juice, sugar, salt and pepper.
- Fruit—as needed—might include limes, lemons, maraschino cherries, cocktail olives, and onions.
- Mixes—a few bottles of soda, tonic, ginger ale.
- Glassware is important to the totality of the cocktail experience. Invest in a few Old-Fashioned glasses (solid, six- to ten-ounce tumblers), collins or highball glasses (reasonably large, eight to twelve ounces), wine glasses (for the cream drinks), a few cognac snifters, and, stem glasses (for those martinis taken straight up).

⌒ Hardware should include a small cutting board and knife, several pour spouts, teaspoon, stirstick (barspoon), swizzle sticks, toothpicks, a sponge or rag, a shot glass, and a martini mixer. A blender is useful for fizzes and other high-calorie concoctions, but it is not absolutely essential for basic cocktails.

Pouring — Pouring drinks is not a complex science—or even very difficult. Fill an empty liquor bottle with water, top with a pour spout, and practice pouring. Grasp the bottle's neck as though it were a door handle, then loop the index finger over one side of the pour spout (to keep it from falling out when you invert the bottle), being careful not to cover the spout's air hole—which will restrict the flow of liquid. To stop the pour, merely rotate your wrist (and the bottle) outward, while raising the pour spout slightly. Do not lift the bottle directly upward to stop, since this method will result in unsightly drips. Use the shot glass to gauge the correct measure.

Floating and Frosting — Glasses can be frosted in the freezer, and they can be chilled in ice or in the refrigerator. Stir drinks two or three times to mix the ingredients. To "float" or layer liquors, pour each individual liquor slowly over the inverted bowl of a teaspoon held about a half-inch above the surface of the drink.

Fruit — A "slice" or "twist" is a sliver cut from the skin of a lemon, lime, or orange. The slice should be "twisted" slightly before going into the drink to release the juices and oils in the skin. A "squeeze" is the juice of a wedge of fruit squeezed into a drink (the squeezed fruit is usually added to the drink). Fruit is generally a garnish added after the liquor and mix.

Measurements — Following are several approximations commonly used in drink recipes. While these may be useful in preparing your first cocktails, you will find that with experience in pouring and measuring cocktails—as in so many other activities—you will acquire a sense of the correct balance to match your individual tastes.

1 pony	=	1 ounce	1 teaspoon	=	1/8 ounce
1 jigger (shot)	=	1 1/2 ounces	1 tablespoon	=	1/2 ounce
1 dash	=	1/6 teaspoon			

Singapore Sling

- ⌣ 1 ounce lemon juice
- ⌣ $\frac{1}{2}$ teaspoon sugar
- ⌣ 1 ounce cherry brandy
- ⌣ 1 ounce gin

Shake well with cracked ice and pour unstrained into 10-ounce glass. Decorate with a slice of orange and a cherry.

Singapore Sling / Sasaki Reflection Goblet

Cuba Libre

- Juice and rind of $1/2$ lime
- 1 $1/2$ — 2 ounces rum

Put lime juice and rind in glass. Add rum.

Fill with club soda and ice cubes.

Cuba Libre / Baccarat Massena Highball Glass

John Collins

- 1 teaspoon sugar dissolved in juice of 1 lemon
- 2 ounces bourbon

Fill with soda over ice cubes while stirring.

John Collins / Orrefors Intermezzo Blue Highball Glass

Planter's Punch

- 1 teaspoon sugar
- 1 1/2 — 2 ounces Jamaican rum
- 1 ounce lemon juice
- 1 splash grenadine
- 2 ounces orange juice

Shake well with fine ice and pour unstrained into 10-ounce glass. Decorate with a slice of lemon, a wedge of lime, and fine orange rind.

Planter's Punch / Rogaska Richmond Highball Glass

Old Fashioned

- 1 lump sugar, saturated with bitters
- Splash of soda
- 1 slice orange, 1 cherry, and ice cubes

Add 1–2 ounces rye or bourbon.

Old Fashioned / Hoya Gothic Spires Double Old Fashioned Glass

Angel's Kiss

- ⌣ Fill 3/4 of liqueur glass with creme de cacao.
- ⌣ Float dollop of heavy cream on liqueur.

Top off with a cherry on a cocktail lance.

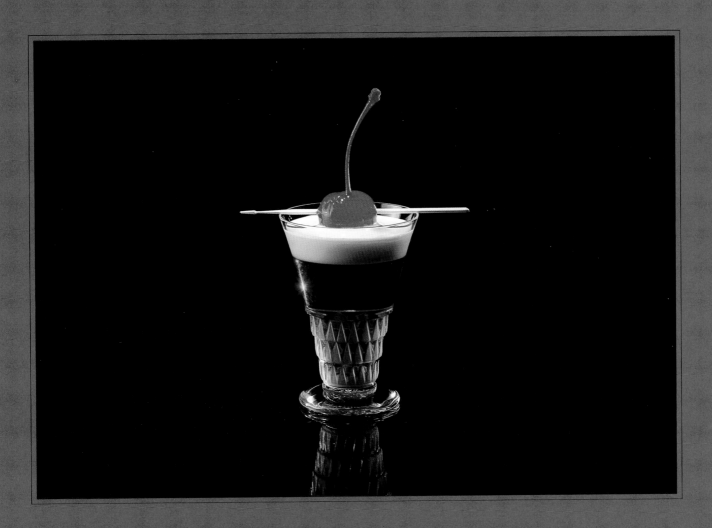

Angel's Kiss / Lalique Bourgueil #6 Liqueur Glass

Eggnog

- 1 teaspoon sugar
- 1 whole egg
- 5 ounces milk
- 1 ½ — 2 ounces rum

Shake with cracked ice and strain.
Sprinkle grated nutmeg on surface.

Eggnog / Hoya Spring Crocus Wine Glass

Mint Julep

- Fresh mint sprigs
- 1 teaspoon sugar
- 1 ½ ounces bourbon
- Splash of soda

Mix sprigs of mint with sugar and splash of soda. Fill 10-ounce glass with fine ice and pour in bourbon. Set glass into container and pack tightly with fine ice. Stir mixture for one minute to freeze outside of glass. Lift out and decorate with two sprigs of mint, slices of orange, and lemon. Powdered sugar over mint adds an optional frosted appearance.

Mint Julep / Italia Metro Highball Glass

Zombie

- 1 ounce lime juice

- 1 ounce lemon juice

- 1 ounce unsweetened pineapple juice

- 1 dash bitters

- 1 1/4 ounces heavy-bodied rum

- 1 1/4 ounces white rum

- 1 1/4 ounces gold rum

Shake with cracked ice and pour unstrained into goblet.
Decorate with fruit.

Zombie / Val St. Lambert Hafnia Goblet

Sidecar

- ⌣ 3/4 ounce brandy
- ⌣ 1/2 ounce lemon juice
- ⌣ 3/4 ounce Cointreau

Rim glass with coarse granulated sugar.

Shake well with cracked ice and strain.

Sidecar / Lalique Argos #4 Wine Glass

Manhattan

- ⌣ 2 ounces rye or bourbon
- ⌣ ½ ounce sweet vermouth
- ⌣ Bitters, if desired

Stir with cracked ice and strain.
Serve with cherry.

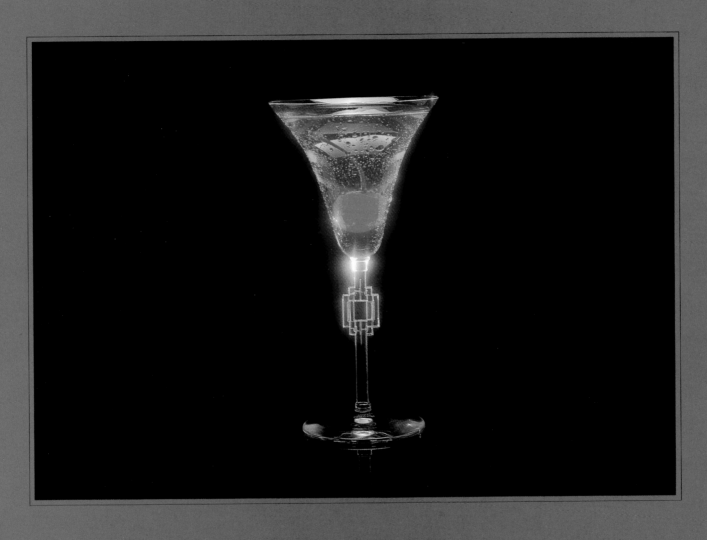

Manhattan / Tosca #4 Wine Glass

Rum Daiquiri

- 1 teaspoon sugar
- 1—2 ounces light rum
- ½ ounce lime juice

Shake well with cracked ice and strain.

Rum Daiquiri / Riedel Exquisite Flute

Stinger

- ⌣ 1 ounce brandy
- ⌣ ¹/₂ ounce white creme de menthe

Shake well with cracked ice and strain.

Stinger / Lalique Orsay #3 Wine Glass

Sloe Gin Fizz

- 1 teaspoon sugar
- 1 ½ ounces lemon juice
- 2 ounces sloe gin

Shake well with cracked ice.

Pour into a highball glass and top with ice-cold soda.

Sloe Gin Fizz / Tommy Highball Glass

Sherry Flip

- 1 teaspoon sugar
- 1 whole egg
- 1—2 ounces sherry

Shake well with cracked ice.

Strain into cocktail glass.

Sprinkle nutmeg on top.

Sherry Flip / Hoya Entasis Wine Glass

Pousse Café

- 1 ounce grenadine
- 1 ounce blue Curaçao
- 1 ounce Bénédictine brandy
- 1 ounce lemon vodka

Pour slowly in stated order over back of spoon into cordial glass.

Pousse Café / Lalique Saint Hubert Cordial Glass

Screwdriver

- ⌣ 1 ½ ounces vodka

- ⌣ 4 ½ ounces freshly squeezed orange juice, ice-cold

- ⌣ 1 teaspoon lemon juice

Pour over ice cubes.

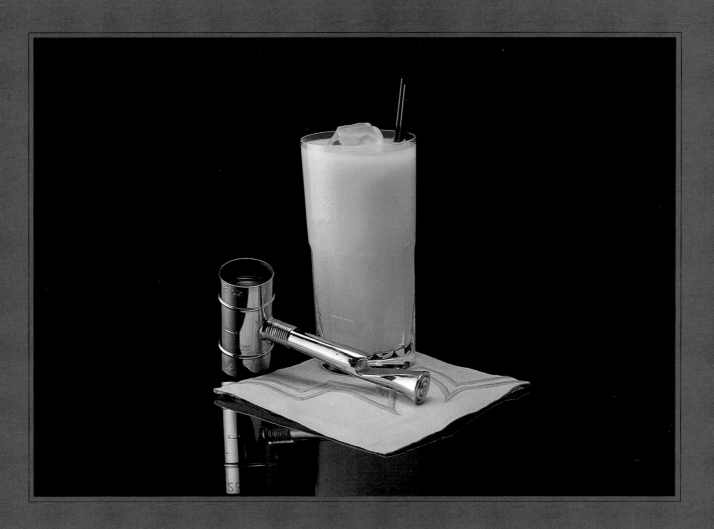

Screwdriver / Saint Louis Bristol Highball Glass

Spencer Cocktail

- 1 dash Angostura bitters
- 1 dash orange juice
- 1 ounce apricot brandy
- 2 ounces dry gin

Shake well and strain into cocktail glass.

Add a cherry.

Spencer Cocktail / Italia Aarne Cocktail Glass

New York Cocktail

- Juice of $\frac{1}{2}$ lime or $\frac{1}{2}$ lemon
- 1 lump sugar
- 2 dashes grenadine
- A twist of orange peel
- 1 $\frac{1}{2}$ ounces whiskey

Shake well and strain into cocktail glass.

New York Cocktail / Waterford Lizmore Cocktail Glass

Apple Brandy Cooler

- 2 ounces brandy
- 1 ounce light rum
- 3 ounces apple juice
- ½ ounce lime juice
- 1 teaspoon dark Jamaican rum

Shake well with ice.

Strain into tall 10-ounce glass.

Float dark rum on surface and add a slice of lime.

Apple Brandy Cooler / Sasaki Cathadia Champagne Flute

Royal Fizz

- ⌣ Juice of $\frac{1}{2}$ lemon
- ⌣ $\frac{1}{2}$ tablespoon powdered sugar
- ⌣ 1 ounce gin
- ⌣ 1 egg

Shake well and strain into 8-ounce glass, then fill with syphon soda water.

Royal Fizz / Hoya Sails Double Old Fashioned Glass

Grasshopper

- 1 ounce green creme de menthe
- 1 ounce white creme de cacao
- 1 ounce heavy cream

Combine and strain through cracked ice.

Grasshopper / Saint Louis Apollo Gold Burgandy Glass

Bloody Mary

- 1 ½ ounces vodka
- 3 ounces tomato juice
- ½ ounce lemon juice
- 1 dash Worcestershire sauce
- 1 dash celery salt
- 1 dash Tabasco sauce

Thoroughly shake all ingredients with ice.

Strain into tall or squat 8-ounce glass.

Decorate with celery.

Bloody Mary / Sasaki Ellessee Double Old Fashioned Glass

Pernod Frappe

- 1 ounce Pernod
- $1/3$ ounce syrup of Anisette plus $2/3$ ounce water.

Shake long enough for the shaker to become thoroughly coated.
Strain into small tumbler.

Pernod Frappe / Hoya Aurora Single Old Fashioned Glass

Margarita

- 1 1/2 ounces tequila
- 1/2 ounce Triple Sec or Curaçao
- 1/2 ounce lemon or lime juice

Shake well with ice.

Strain into pre-chilled, salt-rimmed cocktail glass.

To prepare glass, rub rim with outside of lemon peel then dip into salt, shaking off excess.

A twist of lime or lemon may be added.

Margarita / Lalique Roxane Saucer Champagne Glass

Aquavit Rickey

- 1 ½ ounces Aquavit
- 1 teaspoon dry Kümmel
- ¼ large lime
- Iced club soda

Put 3 ice cubes into an 8-ounce glass.

Add ingredients and stir, leaving lime in glass.

Aquavit Rickey / Sasaki San Marino Champagne Flute

Classic Champagne Cocktail

- ½ teaspoon sugar
- 1 dash Angostura bitters
- 4 ounces iced champagne
- Lemon peel

Stir sugar and bitters in pre-chilled champagne glass.

Add champagne.

Twist lemon peel over and drop into glass.

Classic Champagne Cocktail / Sasaki Renaissance Gold Champagne Flute

Harvey
Wallbanger

- 1 ounce vodka
- $1/4$ ounce Galliano
- 6 ounces orange juice

Shake well and strain into tall glass over ice cubes.

Harvey Wallbanger / Lalique Vigne Champagne Flute

Gimlet Cocktail

- 2 ounces gin

- 2 ounces bottled lime juice

- 1 teaspoon sugar

Stir extremely well with ice.

Strain into pre-chilled cocktail glass.

Sugar frost rim of glass.

Gimlet Cocktail / Lalique Sainte-Odile Specialty Glass

Americano Highball

- 1 ounce Campari bitters
- 2 ounces sweet vermouth

Pour over ice cubes into highball glass.

Fill with soda water.

Add twist of lemon and stir.

Americano Highball / Cristal de Serves Keos Highball Glass

Wedding Belle Cocktail

- ½ ounce orange juice
- ½ ounce cherry brandy
- 1 ounce dry gin
- 1 ounce Dubonnet

Shake well and strain into cocktail glass.

Wedding Belle Cocktail / Hoya Aurora White Wine Glass

Saratoga Cocktail

- 2 dashes grenadine
- 2 dashes Angostura bitters
- 1/4 slice pineapple
- 1 ounce brandy

Shake well and strain.

Add a splash of soda water.

Saratoga Cocktail / Kosta Boda Black Line Cocktail Glass

Frozen Daiquiri

- ½ teaspoon sugar
- ½ ounce lemon juice
- Dash of Maraschino liqueur
- 1 ¼ ounces light rum

Mix with fine cracked ice in mixer or vigorously by hand.

Pour unstrained into champagne saucer.

Top with lime wheel.

Frozen Daiquiri / Baccarat Mercure Saucer Champagne Glass

Rusty Nail

- 1 ounce Scotch whiskey
- 1 ounce Drambuie

Pour over ice cubes and stir.

Rusty Nail / Hoya Aurora Single Old Fashioned Glass

Martini Cocktail

- ⌣ 1/2 — 1 ounce dry vermouth
- ⌣ 2 ounces dry gin

Shake well with ice and strain into martini glass.
Add olive.

Martini Cocktail / Orrefors Intermezzo Blue Martini Glass

Satan's Whiskers Cocktail

- ½ ounce sweet vermouth
- ½ ounce dry vermouth
- ½ ounce gin
- ½ ounce orange juice
- ¼ ounce Grand Marnier
- 1 dash orange bitters

Shake well and strain into cocktail glass.

Satan's Whiskers Cocktail / Rogaska Juliet Goblet

Cinzano Cocktail

- 2 dashes Angostura bitters
- 2 dashes orange bitters
- 2 ounces dry Cinzano vermouth

Shake well and strain into cocktail glass.

Squeeze orange peel on top.

Cinzano Cocktail / Baccarat Martini Glass

Cupid Cocktail

- 2 ounces sherry
- 1 fresh egg
- 1 teaspoon powdered sugar
- A little cayenne pepper

Shake well and strain into medium-size glass.

Cupid Cocktail / Baccarat Brummel Goblet

White Wine Cooler

- 6 ounces chilled white wine
- ½ ounce brandy
- 2 dashes orange bitters
- 1 teaspoon Kümmel
- 2 teaspoons sugar
- ½ ounce lemon juice

Stir into tall 14-ounce glass.

Add a splash of soda and ice cubes to fill glass.

Stir and add long, wide band of cucumber peel.

White Wine Cooler / Baccarat Harmonie Highball Glass

Buckeye Martini

- 2 ½ ounces vodka
- ½ ounce dry vermouth
- 1 large black olive

Stir well and strain into pre-chilled cocktail glass.
Add olive.

Buckeye Martini / Hoya Cut Rock Highball Glass

New Orleans Buck

- 1 ½ ounces light rum
- ½ ounce lime juice
- ½ ounce orange juice
- 2 dashes bitters
- Iced ginger ale

Shake well and strain into 8-ounce glass half-filled with ice.

Add ginger ale and stir.

Add lime slice.

New Orleans Buck / Lalique Bellini Champagne Flute

Chocolate Orange Frappe

- $3/4$ ounce white creme de cacao
- $3/4$ ounce orange juice
- 1 teaspoon Galliano

Stir without ice.

Pour over crushed ice into wine glass.

Chocolate Orange Frappe / Lalique Phalsbourg Wine Glass

Corkscrew

- 1 ½ ounces light rum
- ½ ounce dry vermouth
- ½ ounce peach liqueur
- 1 slice lime

Shake well and strain into pre-chilled cocktail glass.
Add lime slice.

Corkscrew / Riedel Sommelier White Wine Glass

Americana

- 1 teaspoon 100-proof bourbon
- ½ teaspoon sugar
- 1 dash bitters
- 4 ounces iced champagne
- 1 slice fresh peach

Stir bourbon, bitters, and sugar in pre-chilled champagne glass.
Add champagne and peach slice.

Americana / Orrefors Harmony Champagne Flute

Napoleon Cocktail

- 1 dash Fernet Branca
- 1 dash Curaçao
- 1 dash Dubonnet
- 2 ounces dry gin

Shake well and strain into tall glass.

Napoleon Cocktail / Hoya Dimple Highball Glass

Knickerbocker Special Cocktail

- 1 teaspoon raspberry syrup
- 1 teaspoon lemon juice
- 1 teaspoon orange juice
- 1 chunk pineapple
- 2 — 3 ounces light rum
- 2 dashes Curaçao

Shake well and strain into medium-size glass.

Knickerbocker Special Cocktail / Sasaki Tucano Black Wine Glass

Moscow Mule

- 2 ounces vodka
- Wedge of lime
- Iced ginger beer

Pour vodka into 14-ounce glass with ice cubes.

Squeeze lime and drop into glass.

Fill with ginger beer.

Moscow Mule / Italia Aarne Highball Glass

Savoy Hotel
Special Cocktail #2

- 2 dashes Dubonnet
- 1/2 ounce dry vermouth
- 2 ounces dry gin

Shake well with ice and strain into cocktail glass.

Twist orange peel on top.

Savoy Hotel Special Cocktail #2 / Orrefors Cocktail Glass

Bronx Cocktail

- Juice of $1/4$ orange
- $1/2$ ounce dry vermouth
- $1/2$ ounce sweet vermouth
- 1 ounce gin

Shake well and strain into cocktail glass.

Bronx Cocktail / Saint Louis Chantilly Goblet

Black Russian

- 1 ½ ounces vodka
- 3/4 ounce coffee liqueur

Shake well and strain over ice cubes in pre-chilled Old Fashioned glass.

Black Russian / Baccarat Mercure/Neptune Double Old Fashioned Glass

Alabama Fizz

- Juice of 1/2 lemon
- 1/2 tablespoon powdered sugar
- 2 ounces dry gin

Shake well and strain into medium-size glass. Fill with soda water. Add sprigs of fresh mint.

Beer Buster

- 1 1/2 ounces 100-proof vodka
- Ice cold beer
- 2 dashes Tabasco

Pour ingredients into pre-chilled tall 14-ounce glass. Stir lightly.

Bulldog Cocktail

- Juice of 1 orange
- 2 ounces gin
- Ginger ale

Pour juice and gin over ice cubes in large tumbler. Fill with ginger ale and stir. Serve with a straw.

Cape Cod

- 1 1/2 ounces vodka
- 4 1/2 ounces cranberry juice

Shake well and strain into tall 10-ounce glass over ice cubes.

The illustrated cocktails were all mixed with the spirits and liqueurs designated in the recipes by Ryan Sage, Chief Bartender at the Red Car Grill, West Hollywood.

Chartreuse Cooler

- 1 ounce yellow Chartreuse
- 3 ounces orange juice
- 1 ounce lemon juice
- Iced bitter lemon soda

Shake Chartreuse and juices well and strain into tall 14-ounce glass. Fill glass with bitter lemon soda and add orange slice.

Charleston Cocktail

- 1/2 ounce dry gin
- 1/2 ounce kirsch
- 1/2 ounce Maraschino liqueur
- 1/2 ounce Curaçao
- 1/2 ounce dry vermouth
- 1/2 ounce sweet vermouth

Shake well and strain into cocktail glass. Twist lemon peel on top.

Cherry Cobbler

- 1 1/2 ounces gin
- 1/2 ounce Cherry Heering
- 1/2 ounce creme de cassis
- 1 teaspoon sugar
- 1/2 ounce lemon juice
- 1 slice lemon
- 1 maraschino cherry

Stir into 12-ounce glass with finely cracked ice until sugar dissolves. Add lemon slice and cherry.

Cooperstown Cocktail

- 1/2 ounce dry vermouth
- 1/2 ounce sweet vermouth
- 1/2 ounce dry gin

Shake well and strain into cocktail glass. Add a sprig of mint.

Creole

- 1 1/2 ounces light rum
- 1 dash Tabasco
- 1 teaspoon lemon juice
- Iced consommé of beef or beef bouillon
- Salt and pepper

Pour rum, Tabasco, and lemon juice into pre-chilled Old Fashioned glass containing ice cubes. Stir well and add consommé or bouillon. Sprinkle with salt and pepper and stir again.

> "When I was younger I made it a rule never to take a strong drink before lunch. It is now my rule never to do so before breakfast."
>
> -Winston Churchill

Dempsey Cocktail

- 2 dashes Pernod
- 2 dashes grenadine
- 1 ounce gin
- 1 ounce Calvados

Shake well and strain into cocktail glass.

Devil's Tail

- 1 1/2 ounces golden rum
- 1 ounce vodka
- 1/2 ounce lime juice
- 1/4 ounce grenadine
- 1/4 ounce apricot liqueur

Shake well and strain into deep saucer champagne glass filled with crushed ice. Add twist of lime.

> "I never have more than one drink before dinner. But I do like that one to be large and very strong and very well made."
>
> -James Bond

The Earthquake Cocktail

- 1/2 ounce gin
- 1/2 ounce whiskey
- 1/2 ounce Pernod

Shake well and serve in cocktail glass.

Eclipse Cocktail

- Grenadine
- 1 ripe olive
- 1/2 ounce dry gin
- 1 1/2 ounces sloe gin

Pour enough grenadine into a cocktail glass to cover a ripe olive. Mix the spirits together and pour gently over the grenadine so that it does not mix. Twist orange peel on top.

Favorite Cocktail

- 1 dash lemon juice
- 1/2 ounce apricot brandy
- 1/2 ounce dry vermouth
- 1/2 ounce dry gin

Shake well and strain into cocktail glass.

Gibson Cocktail

- 3/4 ounce pre-chilled dry vermouth
- 2 ounces pre-chilled gin

Shake well and strain into pre-chilled cocktail glass. Add small pearl cocktail onion.

Gilroy Cocktail

- 1/2 ounce lemon juice
- 1/2 ounce dry vermouth
- 1 ounce cherry brandy
- 1 ounce dry gin
- 1 dash orange bitters

Shake well and strain into cocktail glass.

Golden Frog

- 1/2 ounce Strega
- 1/2 ounce Galliano
- 1/2 ounce vodka
- 1/2 ounce lemon juice

Shake well and pour into pre-chilled Old Fashioned glass filled with crushed ice.

Greyhound

- 1 1/2 ounces vodka
- 4 1/2 ounces fresh grapefruit juice

Shake well and strain into tall 10-ounce glass over ice cubes.

Highland Cooler

- Juice of 1/2 lemon
- 1 teaspoon powdered sugar
- 2 dashes Angostura bitters
- 1 ounce Scotch whiskey

Pour ingredients into tall glass over ice cubes. Fill with ginger ale.

Honolulu Cocktail

- 1 dash Angostura bitters
- 1 dash orange juice
- 1 dash pineapple juice
- 1 dash lemon juice
- 1 1/2 ounces gin
- A little powdered sugar

Shake well and strain into cocktail glass.

Irish Cocktail

- 2 dashes Pernod
- 2 dashes Curaçao
- 1 dash Maraschino liqueur
- 1 dash Angostura bitters
- 2 ounces Irish whiskey

Shake well and strain into cocktail glass. Add olive and a twist of orange peel on top.

Jack Rose Cocktail

- Juice of 1 lime
- 1/2 ounce grenadine
- 1 1/2 ounces Calvados

Shake well and strain into cocktail glass.

London Buck Cocktail

- Juice of 1/2 lemon
- 2 ounces dry gin
- Ginger ale

Pour ingredients into long tumbler over ice cubes.

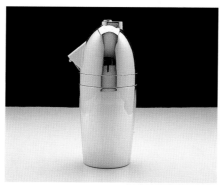

A Soda King syphon designed by Norman Bel Geddes, in chrome-plated metal, manufactured by Walter Kidde Sales Co., Bloomfield, N.J., c. 1935. Various color combinations were also produced.

Maiden's Blush Cocktail

- 1 dash lemon juice
- 4 dashes orange Curaçao
- 4 dashes grenadine
- 1 1/2 ounces dry gin

Shake well and strain into cocktail glass.

Mimosa

- 1 1/2 ounces fresh orange juice
- Pre-chilled champagne

Pour champagne over orange juice to fill pre-chilled champagne glass.

Mississippi Mule Cocktail

- 1 1/2 ounce dry gin
- 1/2 ounce lemon juice
- 1/2 ounce creme de cassis

Shake well and strain into cocktail glass.

Monte Carlo Imperial Cocktail

- 1 ounce dry gin
- 1 ounce lemon juice
- 1/2 ounce creme de menthe
- Chilled champagne

Shake gin, lemon juice, and creme de menthe and strain into medium-size glass. Fill with champagne.

A chromed-metal cocktail shaker in the shape of a Graf von Zeppelin airship, c. 1925, manufactured in Germany.

Mule's Hind Leg Cocktail

- ½ ounce gin
- ½ ounce Bénédictine brandy
- ½ ounce Applejack
- 2 ounces maple syrup
- ½ ounce apricot brandy

Shake well and strain into cocktail glass.

Olympic Cocktail

- 1 ounce orange juice
- 1 ounce Curaçao
- 1 ounce brandy

Shake well and strain into cocktail glass.

Opera Cocktail

- ½ ounce Maraschino liqueur
- ½ ounce Dubonnet
- 1 ½ ounces dry gin

Shake well and strain into cocktail glass. Add a squeeze of orange peel on top.

Oriental Cocktail

- Juice of ½ lime
- 1 ounce rye whiskey
- ½ ounce sweet vermouth
- ½ ounce white Curaçao

Shake well and strain into cocktail glass.

Parisian Cocktail

- 1 ounce dry vermouth
- 1 ounce creme de cassis
- 1 ounce gin

Shake well and strain into cocktail glass.

Peter Pan Cocktail

- ½ ounce bitters
- ½ ounce orange juice
- ½ ounce dry vermouth
- ½ ounce dry gin

Shake well and strain into cocktail glass.

Pineapple Fizz

- 2 tablespoons pineapple juice
- ½ tablespoon powdered sugar
- 2 ounces light rum

Shake well and strain into 8-ounce glass. Fill with soda water.

Pousse Café #2

- 1 ounce grenadine
- 1 ounce creme de menthe
- 1 ounce green Chartreuse
- 2 ounces cognac

Pour slowly in stated order over back of spoon into cordial glass.

Queen's Cocktail

- ½ slice pineapple, crushed
- ½ ounce dry vermouth
- ½ ounce sweet vermouth
- 1 ounce gin

Shake well and strain into cocktail glass.

Raquet Club Cocktail

- 1 dash orange bitters
- ½ ounce dry vermouth
- 1 ½ ounces pink gin

Shake well and strain into cocktail glass.

Russian Bear

- 1 ounce vodka
- ½ ounce creme de cacao
- ½ ounce cream

Shake well and strain into cocktail glass.

Shanghai Cocktail

- 2 dashes grenadine
- 1 ounce lemon juice
- ¼ ounce Pernod
- 1 ounce Jamiacan rum

Shake well and strain into cocktail glass.

The contents include a shaker, decanter, reamer, strainer, four shot glasses, a funnel, four swizzle spoons, and a corkscrew. These are compactly housed in specifically designed compartments with characteristic German precision.

> "The only time I ever said no to a drink was when I misunderstood the question."
>
> -Will Sinclair

Southern Gin Cocktail

- 2 dashes Curaçao
- 2 dashes orange bitters
- 2 ounces dry gin

Shake well and strain into cocktail glass.

Tempter Cocktail

- 1 ounce port wine
- 1 ounce apricot brandy

Shake well and strain into cocktail glass.

Thunder and Lightning Cocktail

- 1 egg yolk
- 1 ½ ounces brandy
- 1 teaspoon powdered sugar

Shake well and strain into 1 0-ounce glass. Add a dash of cayenne pepper on top.

Tom and Jerry

- 1 egg
- ½ ounce Jamaican rum
- 1 tablespoon powdered sugar
- ½ ounce brandy

Beat egg white and yolk separately. Mix yolk and white together and pour into stemmed glass. Add spririts. Fill with boiling water and grate nutmeg on top.

Torpedo Cocktail

- 1 dash gin
- ½ ounce brandy
- 1 ½ ounces Calvados

Shake well and strain into cocktail glass.

Tropical Cocktail

- 1 dash Angostura bitters
- 1 dash orange bitters
- 1 ounce creme de cacao
- 1 ounce Maraschino liqueur
- 1 ounce dry vermouth

Shake well and strain into cocktail glass.

Vodka Stinger

- 1 ½ ounces vodka
- 1 ½ ounces creme de menthe

Shake extremely well and strain into pre-chilled cocktail glass.

Vodka Fraise

- 3/4 ounce vodka
- 3/4 ounce light rum
- 1/2 ounce strawberry liqueur
- 1/2 ounce lime juice
- 1/2 teaspoon grenadine

Shake well and strain into pre-chilled sugar-rimmed cocktail glass. Float 1/2 large strawberry on surface.

Warsaw Cocktail

- 1 1/2 ounces vodka
- 1/2 ounce blackberry liqueur
- 1/2 ounce dry vermouth
- 1 teaspoon lemon juice

Shake well and strain into pre-chilled cocktail glass. Add twist of lemon.

A cocktail shaker by Revere, 1937. The Skyscraper shaker dominates a Manhattan tray and chrome goblets. The tray and shaker were designed by Norman Bel Geddes.

Whiskey Daisy

- 1 1/2 ounces blended whiskey
- 1 teaspoon red currant syrup
- 1/2 ounce lemon juice
- 1 teaspoon yellow Chartreuse
- Club soda

Shake whiskey, syrup, and lemon juice well and strain into 8-ounce glass. Add soda and stir. Float Chartreuse on top and decorate with slice of lemon.

White Russian

- 1 ounce vodka
- 1 ounce coffee liqueur
- 3 1/2 ounces fresh cream or milk

Pour ingredients over ice cubes in a 10-ounce tall glass and stir.

Widow's Dream Cocktail

- 1 egg
- 1 1/2 ounces Bénédictine brandy

Shake well and strain into medium-sized glass. Fill with cream.

> "If people are injured from the use of liquor, the injury arises not from the use of a bad thing, but from the abuse of a good thing."
>
> -Abraham Lincoln

Will Rogers Cocktail

- 1/2 ounce orange juice
- 1/2 ounce dry vermouth
- 1/2 ounce dry gin
- 1 ounce Curaçao

Shake well and strain into cocktail glass.

Zaza Cocktail

- 1 ounce Dubonnet
- 1 ounce gin

Shake well and strain into cocktail glass.

The bar at the Red Car Grill, West Hollywood.

Acknowledgments

Grateful thanks are due to Harvey and Mark Schwartz, Frank Piccolo, Kay Tornborg, Mary Merrick, Eric Menard, Peter Linden, Kirk Giroux, Robert Silva and the cheerful staff at Gump's, Beverly Hills, Steve Shern and Alison Sklute. Particular thanks are due to Steve Grant and Ryan Sage at the Red Car Grill, and to Sam Sargent.

All glassware illustrated in this book was kindly loaned by Gump's, Beverly Hills.

Credits:

P.6 Miniatures: Courtesy The Wine Shop, Los Angeles.

P.11 High hat shaker and jigger: Courtesy Eric Menard and Peter Linden.

P.13 Chase drum ashtray and muddler: Courtesy Eric Menard and Peter Linden.

P.15 Chase top hat jigger and mixer: Courtesy Eric Menard and Peter Linden.

P.17 Chase mixer: Courtesy Eric Menard and Peter Linden. Nut dish: Courtesy Kay Tornborg.

P.19 Chase drum cigarette server: Courtesy Eric Menard and Peter Linden. Matchbox: Courtesy L.J.P. Props. Cocktail napkin: Courtesy Gump's, Beverly Hills.

P.27 Cocktail napkin: Courtesy Gump's, Beverly Hills.

P.29 Cocktail tray, cigarettes, and matchbook: Courtesy L.J.P. Props. Chase swan ashtray: Courtesy Eric Menard and Peter Linden .

P.33 Cocktail napkin: Courtesy Gump's, Beverly Hills.

P.35 Cocktail napkin: Courtesy Red Car Grill.

P.37 Zeppelin shaker: Courtesy Piccolo Pete's, Sherman Oaks. Cocktail napkin: Courtesy Gump's, Beverly Hills. Mixer: Courtesy Steve Shern.

P.39 Cocktail tray: Courtesy L.J.P. Props. Chase bell and vase: Courtesy Eric Menard and Peter Linden.

P.43 Cocktail napkin: Courtesy Kay Tornborg. Chase jigger and opener: Courtesy Piccolo Pete's, Sherman Oaks.

P.45 Clock and table lighter: Courtesy L.J.P. Props. Cherry spoon: Courtesy Kay Tornborg.

P.47 High hat mixer: Courtesy Eric Menard and Peter Linden. Shaker: Courtesy Piccolo Pete's, Sherman Oaks.

P.51 Dominos: Courtesy L.J.P. Props. Chase muddler: Courtesy Eric Menard and Peter Linden.

P.53 Grasshoppers: Courtesy Kay Tornborg.

P.57 Catalin poker chips: Courtesy L.J.P. Props. Chase ashtray and playing cards: Courtesy Eric Menard and Peter Linden.

P.59 Chase server: Courtesy Eric Menard and Peter Linden. Cocktail napkin: Courtesy Kay Tornborg.

P.61 Cocktail napkin: Courtesy Kay Tornborg.

P.63 Chase drum desk lamp: Courtesy Eric Menard and Peter Linden.

P.65 Cocktail tray and cigarettes: Courtesy L.J.P. Props. Nut server: Courtesy Gump's, Beverly Hills.

P.67 Chase pretzel holder: Courtesy Eric Menard and Peter Linden. Cocktail napkin: Courtesy Gump's, Beverly Hills.

P.69 Cigarettes: Courtesy L.J.P. Props. Striker and matches: Courtesy Robert Amram.

P.71 Cocktail napkin: Courtesy Gump's, Beverly Hills.

P.73 Game board and pieces: Courtesy Kay Tornborg. Dice: Courtesy Harvey's, Melrose Avenue.

P.75 Radio: Courtesy L.J.P. Props.

P.77 Cocktail napkin: Courtesy Gump's, Beverly Hills. Chase muddler: Courtesy Eric Menard and Peter Linden.

P.79 Swan olive-pick server: Courtesy Harvey's, Melrose Avenue.

P.81 Ashtray: Courtesy Kay Tornborg.

P.83 Turntable and record: Courtesy L.J.P. Props.

P.85 Valentine card: Courtesy Kay Tornborg.

P.87 Fan: Courtesy L.J.P. Props.

P.89 Olive server: Eric Menard and Peter Linden. Olive pick: Courtesy Harvey's, Melrose Avenue.

P.91 Chase mixer: Courtesy Eric Menard and Peter Linden.

P.95 Corkscrews: Courtesy Harvey's, Melrose Avenue.

P.97 Clock: Courtesy L.J.P. Props. Nut server: Courtesy Eric Menard and Peter Linden.

P.99 Lucite chess set: Courtesy Harvey's, Melrose Avenue. Chess board: Courtesy Kay Tornborg.

P.101 Telephone: Courtesy L.J.P. Props. Numbers index: Courtesy Off the Wall, Los Angeles.

P.103 Pravda newspaper: Courtesy L.J.P. Props.

P.105 Books: Courtesy L.J.P. Props.

P.107 Cocktail shaker: Courtesy Harvey's, Melrose Avenue. Cocktail napkin: Courtesy Gump's, Beverly Hills.

P.109 Cigarettes box and passport: Courtesy L.J.P. Props.

P.113 Soda King Syphon: Courtesy Harvey's, Melrose Avenue.

P.114-115 Zeppelin shaker: Courtesy Piccolo Pete's, Sherman Oaks.

P.116 Shaker, glasses and tray: Courtesy Eric Menard and Peter Linden.

Index